SMART STRATEGIES FOR SHARING, SUBLETTING, AND RENTING AN APARTMENT

FINANCIAL SECURITY AND
LIFE SUCCESS FOR TEENS™

SMART STRATEGIES FOR
SHARING, SUBLETTING, AND RENTING AN APARTMENT

JENNIFER LANDAU

ROSEN
PUBLISHING®

New York

Published in 2015 by The Rosen Publishing Group, Inc.
29 East 21st Street, New York, NY 10010

Library of Congress Cataloging-in-Publication Data

Landau, Jennifer, 1961–
Smart strategies for sharing, subletting, and renting an apartment/Jennifer Landau.
    pages cm.—(Financial security and life success for teens)
Includes bibliographical references and index.
Audience: Grade 7–12.
ISBN 978-1-4777-7630-8 (library bound)—ISBN 978-1-4777-7632-2 (pbk.)—
ISBN 978-1-4777-7633-9 (6-pack)
1. Apartments—United States—Juvenile literature. 2. Rental housing—United States—Juvenile literature. 3. Subleases—United States—Juvenile literature. 4. Landlord and tenant—United States—Juvenile literature. 5. House buying—United States—Juvenile literature. I. Title.
HD7287.6.U5L28 2015
643'.27—dc23

                                      2013046611

Manufactured in China

CONTENTS

INTRODUCTION

From the late 1990s to the mid-2000s, there was a housing boom in the United States. Spurred on by a strong economy and government incentives, many Americans bought houses and apartments they couldn't afford with loans they were unable to pay back. Many of these people were allowed to take out loans without putting any money down or having any kind of credit check. They had to pay a higher interest rate on their loans, which made lenders all the more anxious to have them sign on the dotted line. There was even a practice called robo-signing, where lenders signed off on loans without reading them or faked a signature to push the loan through.

For a time, housing prices continued to rise. According to the Case-Schiller Home Price Index, home values more than doubled in twenty major cities between 2000 and 2006. By the late 2000s, however, the boom went bust. Home prices dropped, the economy faltered, and unemployment rose. This left many borrowers unable to pay back their loans. Millions foreclosed on these homes, which means that the lender took possession of the home because the owner was no longer able to make payments.

Although these conditions caused hardship for many, some tough lessons were learned. People can no longer take out loans with no money down and bad credit. Lenders are asking for 10 to 20 percent for a down payment and typically six months cash reserve in the bank. They are analyzing

Whether you are renting or buying an apartment, you need to take ownership of the process. Only then will you be able to enjoy and succeed in your new living situation.

financial records such as bank statements, pay stubs, and W-2 forms, and checking out how much debt a potential owner is carrying. People, especially young adults, have realized that renting an apartment or house often makes a lot more financial sense than buying one, at least in the short term. Landlords have become equally cautious, however, unwilling to rent an apartment to someone who is not in good financial shape. This might feel like a burden, but it is really a blessing. If you get in over your head, not only will you not enjoy your home, you will likely have to endure the trauma of being forced out of it.

It's far better to be realistic from the start, to know your priorities when it comes to housing, and to find a place that lets you enjoy your home without breaking the bank. It's also important to take ownership of the process, whether you are renting or buying an apartment. Turning to experts for advice is a smart idea, but it doesn't replace the need for you to do your own research and take stock of your particular needs before you make a move. Your real estate agent, landlord, or lender will not be living in your apartment. This will be *your* place. If you take the steps outlined here, you'll be well on your way to making that apartment one you're happy to call home.

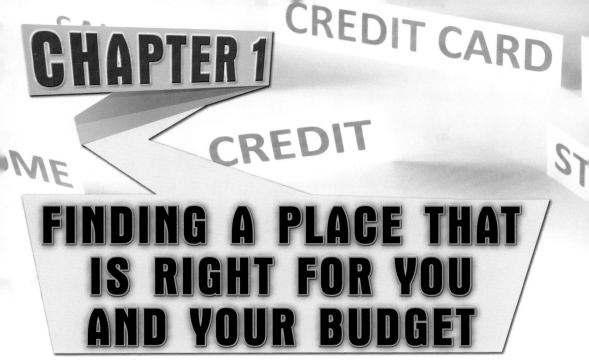

CHAPTER 1

FINDING A PLACE THAT IS RIGHT FOR YOU AND YOUR BUDGET

In her book *The Money Class*, financial expert Suze Orman offers the following advice to her readers: "Stand in your truth." She defines this as a "painfully honest, clear-eyed stock-taking of your personal finances, as well as your dreams for the future."

For many people starting out in life, the truth is that buying an apartment is just not possible—yet. When you're fresh from college or new to the working world, it is rare to have the financial means to buy an apartment. In order to buy, you have to make a down payment, which is money you give a bank or other lender to lower the amount you'll owe when you take out a loan for the rest. If you want to buy an apartment that costs $125,000 for example, and the down payment is 10 percent of the total price, you will need to have $12,500 on hand, in cash, for the down payment.

You'll also have to make monthly payments on your mortgage, which is the loan you take out to buy the property. There are many other potential costs as well, such as attorney fees

Not many people starting out in life can afford to buy an apartment. Renting is a good way to save money and give yourself time to figure out your long-term goals.

or the fee to have the apartment inspected to make sure it is in tip-top shape. Big purchases tend to be a big drain on your bank account, and buying a home of any sort is one of life's big purchases.

There is no shame in renting, however. It is far better to live within your means—or, better yet, below your means— than to reach to acquire something you simply can't afford. After the housing collapse of the late 2000s, people are now more careful about how they spend their money. Spending less and saving more is now seen as a smart move. As Marianne Cusato, author of *The Just Right Home*, puts it: "Austerity is the new bling."

THE SEVEN-YEAR PLAN

It's not just money that makes the difference in whether you rent or buy. It's the phase of life you're going through, too. As a young person, you might want more freedom to live in different parts of the country or in different cities in the state you've called home for years. You might want to wait to see how your work life progresses or whether you want to get additional education. Perhaps you've yet to meet the person you want to spend your life with and want to wait until you're in a committed relationship to think about buying an apartment. Renting simply offers more flexibility and freedom to change direction than buying ever can.

One thing to think about when deciding whether to buy or rent an apartment is your seven-year plan. What do you want your work life to look like in seven years? Your social life? Do you see yourself in an urban setting or a suburban one? A high-rise building or a townhouse? Is saving money for travel a bigger priority than saving for an apartment? What steps are you going to take to make these dreams of yours come true?

If the mere idea of having a seven-year plan makes you break out in a sweat, then you're probably not ready to

THE BOOMERANG GENERATION

IT'S AN ECONOMIC REALITY. IF YOU CAN'T FIND A JOB THAT PAYS ENOUGH TO LIVE ON YOUR OWN, OR IF YOU LOSE YOUR JOB OR SOME OTHER HARDSHIP HITS, YOU MIGHT END UP HAVING TO STAY WITH YOUR PARENTS. THERE'S EVEN A TERM FOR THIS: THE BOOMERANG GENERATION. ACCORDING TO A RECENT POLL BY PEW RESEARCH, 29 PERCENT OF PARENTS REPORT THAT THEIR YOUNG ADULT CHILDREN ARE LIVING WITH THEM. PERHAPS MORE SURPRISINGLY, A LARGE MAJORITY (78 PERCENT) OF THESE CHILDREN REPORTED THAT THEY FELT SATISFIED WITH THEIR LIVING ARRANGEMENTS.

AN IMPORTANT POINT TO HIGHLIGHT IS THESE YOUNG ADULTS HAD A FINANCIAL STAKE IN THE RUNNING OF THE HOUSEHOLD. FORTY-EIGHT PERCENT SAID THEY PAID RENT, WHILE 89 PERCENT SAID THEY HELPED WITH HOUSEHOLD EXPENSES. EXPECTING YOUR PARENTS TO PAY FOR EVERYTHING IS UNFAIR TO THEM AND WILL LIKELY CAUSE YOUR SELF-ESTEEM TO TAKE A HIT. YOU DON'T WANT TO TAKE ADVANTAGE OF THEIR HOSPITALITY, AND YOU *DO* WANT TO FEEL AS IF PAYING YOUR OWN WAY IS A REAL POSSIBILITY FOR THE FUTURE.

BESIDES CONTRIBUTING TO EXPENSES, OFFER TO HELP WITH CHORES AROUND THE HOUSE TO LET YOUR PARENTS KNOW YOU APPRECIATE THEIR GENEROSITY. IF YOU'RE CONCERNED ABOUT NOT BEING TREATED LIKE AN ADULT, YOU COULD EVEN WRITE UP A CONTRACT STATING HOW MUCH YOU'LL PAY IN RENT, HOW MUCH YOU'LL CONTRIBUTE TO EXPENSES, AND ANY OTHER POSSIBLE STICKING POINTS. YOU SHOULD ALSO AVOID SEEING THIS STAY AS PERMANENT OR YOUR PARENTS AS A RESCUE SQUAD. SAVE YOUR MONEY AND COME UP WITH A STEP-BY-STEP PLAN TO MOVE TOWARD FINANCIAL INDEPENDENCE — AND OUT OF YOUR PARENTS' HOUSE.

buy more than a couch and some curtains. There's nothing wrong with that. Everyone goes through life at his or her own pace, and taking the time to figure out what you want is far better than rushing into something because you think you should or because everyone around you seems to be moving at a faster clip than you are.

When you rent, you have the freedom to move every year or two to suit the changes in your work or personal life. Having your own place also allows you greater freedom to develop the kind of social life you want.

CALCULATING THE COSTS

For those who are now renting and want to decide if buying is a better financial deal, there are many tools to help them figure that out. The *New York Times* has a rent versus buy calculator (http://www.nytimes.com/interactive/business/buy-rent-calculator.html?_r=0) that lets you put in information such as your monthly rent, the price of the apartment you are thinking of buying, the down payment on that apartment, and the mortgage rate, which is the percent of interest on your mortgage. Then the calculator shows whether buying or renting makes more financial sense after a certain amount of time. There is even a graph that gives you a clear visual to help you see the difference.

As an example, if you currently pay $1,200 per month in rent, want to buy a $125,000 apartment, and put a down payment of 10 percent of the entire cost ($12,500) at a rate of 5.5 percent of interest on the mortgage, buying will cost less than renting after three years, with an average savings of $5,054 per year.

One big distinction between renting and buying is that when you rent, the amount you pay is subject to inflation. This means that if there is a general rise in prices, your landlord will likely charge you more in rent. If you buy, the price of your apartment

There are tools available to help you calculate whether it makes more financial sense to rent or buy. It's important to be realistic when deciding what you can afford.

DIFFERENT TYPES OF LIVING SPACES

THERE ARE MANY DIFFERENT KINDS OF APARTMENTS FROM WHICH YOU CAN CHOOSE.

Mid-Rise or High-Rise Building

MID-RISE OR HIGH-RISE BUILDINGS ARE MOST LIKELY FOUND IN URBAN SETTINGS. MID-RISE BUILDINGS ARE FIVE TO TEN STORIES HIGH, WHILE HIGH-RISE BUILDINGS ARE MORE THAN TEN STORIES HIGH. THESE DWELLINGS RANGE FROM LUXURY BUILDINGS TO LOWER-END RESIDENCES IN THE INNER CITY.

Town House

A TOWN HOUSE IS A SINGLE-FAMILY HOME ATTACHED TO OTHER HOMES ON BOTH SIDES. TOWN HOUSES ARE THREE TO FIVE STORIES AND ARE OFTEN FOUND ON THE OUTSKIRTS OF A CITY CENTER. IN MANY TOWN HOUSES, THE FIRST FLOOR IS RAISED ABOVE STREET LEVEL, WHICH ALLOWS THE BASEMENT LEVEL TO GET SOME LIGHT.

Loft

LOFTS, FOUND IN URBAN AREAS, ARE KNOWN FOR THEIR OPEN FLOOR PLANS. LOFTS ALLOW FOR FLEXIBLE LIVING SITUATIONS AND CAN HAVE GREAT CHARM. THERE IS OFTEN INTENSE COMPETITION FOR THESE UNIQUE APARTMENTS.

APARTMENT HOUSE

AN APARTMENT HOUSE CONTAINS A SMALL NUMBER OF UNITS, WITH SOME BUILDINGS LOOKING LIKE SINGLE-FAMILY HOMES. THEY ARE MAKING A COMEBACK IN URBAN AREAS WITH DEVELOPMENTS SPRINGING UP IN OLDER, PREVIOUSLY NEGLECTED NEIGHBORHOODS.

APARTMENT COMPLEX

AN APARTMENT COMPLEX CONTAINS A LARGE NUMBER OF BUILDINGS CENTERED AROUND PARKING LOTS AND COMMUNAL OUTDOOR AREAS. THESE APARTMENTS ARE OFTEN AVAILABLE, AND MANY ARE RENTALS. AS EACH BEDROOM OFTEN HAS A BATHROOM ATTACHED, THIS CAN BE A GOOD PICK IF YOU WILL HAVE ROOMMATES.

remains the same. Your $125,000 apartment won't suddenly cost you $150,000 because overall prices have gone up. If the economy is strong, however, and you stay in the apartment for at least a few years, you can usually count on making a profit when it's time to sell because the value of the apartment will have risen. Since the apartment is now worth more, you can sell it for more than you originally paid to buy it.

An owner is also building up equity on his or her apartment. Equity is the difference between what someone would pay for your apartment (called its market value) and the amount of money you still owe on your loan. If your apartment has a market value of $150,000 and you owe your lender $100,000, you have $50,000 worth of equity in your home.

A PLACE OF YOUR OWN

Another difference between renting and owning is that when you own an apartment, you can do whatever you like with it. You can paint the walls green or turn the second bedroom into a man cave or anything else you want without having to

An advantage to owning an apartment is that you can make changes such as painting a room a different color without having to get permission from a landlord.

ask the landlord's permission. Although some landlords are great, others seem determined to make their tenants' lives miserable. Not having to answer to anyone but yourself or someone you've chosen to live with can be a real plus. Even as an apartment owner, however, you probably shouldn't be too outrageous when you make changes. Some day you might want to sell your apartment, and you'll have to redo any extreme wall colors or other interior designs to avoid losing a potential buyer.

While not having a landlord offers you some leeway, it also means taking care of everything yourself. If the toilet backs up or the refrigerator breaks down, it's up to you to get it fixed. There's a lot of pride that comes from owning your own apartment. But there's a lot of responsibility that comes with it, too.

CHAPTER 2

GETTING YOUR FINANCES IN ORDER

When you're planning a move, you need to know not just how much it costs to rent or buy an apartment, but also how much money you have available to spend. Start with what you earn. How big is your paycheck? How often do you get paid? How much is taken out for taxes? If you need help understanding your paycheck, Paycheckcity.com has a free calculator to help you figure out what it all means.

Then it's time to zero in on your expenses. There are Web sites and apps that can help you with this, but a pen and paper will do fine, too. What's important is to keep track of your expenses over at least a three-month period to see how much you spend in an average month. These costs include:

• Housing
• Taxes
• Transportation
• Food (including eating out at restaurants)
• Health care
• Debt (credit cards, student loans, car loans)
• Appearance (clothing, haircuts, jewelry)
• Entertainment

As you keep track of your monthly expenses, don't forget to include nonessentials like that daily latte or a gym membership.

- Travel
- Educational costs
- Incidentals: Miscellaneous expenses such as birthday, wedding, or baby gifts; dry cleaning; and gym memberships.

STICKER SHOCK

Many people are amazed at how much they spend each month. Depending on how far away from your job you live, transportation costs can really eat away at your paycheck. According to CommuteSolutions.com, a Web site run by the Santa Cruz County Regional Transportation Commission, a person who commutes by car 60 miles (97 kilometers) per day five days per week ends up spending nearly $20,000 a year

Transportation costs can make up a large part of your monthly expenses. Driving 60 miles (97 kilometers) to and from work every weekday can cost nearly $20,000 a year.

driving to and from work! Another shocker is the amount spent on nonessentials like cappuccinos, electronic gadgets, and Netflix accounts. Although no one should live a life of all work and no play, it's important to take a hard look at just how much all that play is costing you.

To reach your financial goals, you should save a minimum of 10 percent of your pretax income. You should be thinking not only of your housing costs, but also of the money you'll need in the years to come for retirement and other concerns. No one has a crystal ball to predict what programs such as Social Security and Medicare will look like in years to come. What is certain is that everyone hits a bump in the road in his or her life, whether that is a job loss, an unexpected health expense, or some other difficulty. You don't have to put away every dollar in preparation for a disaster, but you shouldn't act recklessly, either. You should create and maintain a financial cushion to keep you afloat in sudden emergencies or downturns.

DEBT CRISIS

A sure way to save money is to lower your debt. Credit cards, for example, encourage you to live beyond your means and can lead you to make impulse purchases that you might regret later. These cards have high interest rates and are not tax-deductible, so the full weight of the debt falls on you. If you can't pay off your credit cards all at once, switch to ones with lower interest rates and focus on reducing your spending.

Pay attention to your spending habits, too. Perhaps a debit card would serve you better if the temptation to reach for your credit card proves too strong. Debit cards look like credit cards, but the money is taken directly from your checking account within a day or two. Living independently, whether renting or buying, requires discipline and sound judgment, so facing your debt head on is a great place to start.

One huge source of debt is college loans. According to the Consumer Financial Protection Bureau, student loan debt in the United States has topped more than $1 trillion! On top of that, a report by the Federal Reserve Bank of New York shows that nearly a third of these borrowers are behind in paying back their loans. This debt leaves young people less able to take care of their present needs, including housing. Jed Kolko, chief economist at Trulia, a real estate Web site, told the *New York Times* that "[h]aving a lot of student loan debt makes it harder to qualify for a mortgage and harder to save for a down payment."

While college is seen as a smart investment in the long run, anyone taking out a student loan should be clear about the dollars and cents involved. The interest rates on loans can vary widely, depending on both the financial and governmental climate. In 2011, the average college loan debt was $23,300 according to a National Reserve Bank of New York report, with 10 percent of graduates owing more than $54,000. Even public universities, which are run by individual states and charge their residents lower tuition than private colleges, have added to this debt burden. According to the Department of Education, by 2016,

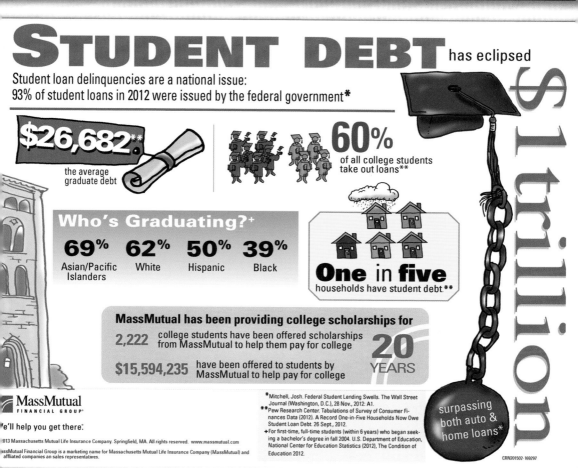

STUDENT DEBT has eclipsed

Student loan delinquencies are a national issue:
93% of student loans in 2012 were issued by the federal government*

$26,682** the average graduate debt

60% of all college students take out loans**

Who's Graduating?+

69% Asian/Pacific Islanders **62%** White **50%** Hispanic **39%** Black

One in five households have student debt.**

MassMutual has been providing college scholarships for

2,222 college students have been offered scholarships from MassMutual to help them pay for college

$15,594,235 have been offered to students by MassMutual to help pay for college

20 YEARS

MassMutual
FINANCIAL GROUP*

We'll help you get there.

©2013 Massachusetts Mutual Life Insurance Company. Springfield, MA. All rights reserved. www.massmutual.com
MassMutual Financial Group is a marketing name for Massachusetts Mutual Life Insurance Company (MassMutual) and affiliated companies an sales representatives.

*Mitchell, Josh. Federal Student Lending Swells. The Wall Street Journal (Washington, D.C.), 28 Nov., 2012: A1.
**Pew Research Center. Tabulations of Survey of Consumer Finances Data (2012). A Record One-in-Five Households Now Owe Student Loan Debt. 26 Sept., 2012.
+For first-time, full-time students (within 6 years) who began seeking a bachelor's degree in fall 2004. U.S. Department of Education, National Center for Education Statistics (2012), The Condition of Education 2012.

CRN201502-169297

$1 trillion

surpassing both auto & home loans*

One in five households has student loan debt. The total debt in the United States has reached more than $1 trillion, creating a crisis situation.

tuition at state schools will be *double* what it was fifteen years earlier.

The combination of people hungry for college, easy-to-secure government loans, and schools that encourage their students not to worry about the price of their education until later can

REIGNING IN YOUR SPENDING

If you're trying to trim the fat in your budget, consider these money-saving tips:

- Bring lunch to work, rather than eating out.
- Buy generic brands, rather than name brands. You'll likely get equal quality for a lower price.
- Drop luxuries such as the newest version of a gadget you already own.
- Buy used items. This can make a huge difference, especially with big-ticket items such as cars.
- Use public transportation more often. It's cheaper than driving and better for the environment, too.
- Exercise at home or in the park, rather than joining a gym.
- If you're tempted to buy an expensive item, force yourself to wait forty-eight hours before making the purchase. It just might not seem so inviting once you've had a couple of days to think about it.
- Research free sources of entertainment. Instead of paying for movies or a concert, find out about free concerts, plays, or readings. Rent DVDs from the library instead of paying for services like Netflix or Hulu.
- When it comes to travel, use Internet sites to find the best deal. Travel during off-peak hours and plan your vacation away from major holidays.

create a crisis situation. "I readily admit it," E. Gordon Gee, president of Ohio State University told the *New York Times*. "I do not think we have given significant thought to the impact of college costs on families." You can't afford to do the same.

KNOW THE SCORE

If you plan on renting or buying an apartment, your credit score will have a huge impact on that process. An unfavorable credit report will affect whether you can get a mortgage (and at what interest rate) or whether a landlord is willing to risk taking you on as a tenant.

The credit score was first developed by the Fair Isaac Corporation, which is why it is also known as a FICO score. This score is a number between 300 and 850 that tells a landlord or lender your credit history, including the types of credit you use, how long you've had each of your accounts open, and whether you've paid your bills on time. The credit score also includes information from your public record, such as whether you've had an unpaid debt sent to a collection agency, had money taken from your paycheck for failure to repay a debt, or declared bankruptcy. These are black marks on your credit history and will have a negative effect on how you fare in the real estate market.

As with many grades, the higher your credit score is, the better. There are three credit reporting agencies—Equifax, Experian, and Transunion—that offer free reports once a year so that you can check your credit. In some cases, you have to pay a small fee to get your actual credit score. It's important to get all three reports, as each may be slightly different.

Why bother to check your credit report if the information contained within it is already out there, available for any land-lord or mortgage officer to peruse? That information could be

The Federal Trade Commission (FTC) recommends that you look over your credit report once a year. Any mistake or inaccuracy could affect your credit score and impact your ability to get an apartment.

inaccurate, incomplete, or even associated with someone else entirely who shares your name. If you do find an error, it's up to the credit reporting agency to investigate and get back to you within thirty days.

In the cases in which the negative information is correct, you can work to raise your credit score, although it will not happen overnight. Ways to do this include paying down your debt, not applying for new credit cards, and paying all your bills on time. If you're late with a payment, don't wait until the next billing cycle to pay, as you will then be thirty days late, which will lower your credit score even more. These small steps can make a big difference in how your rental or home loan application is received when it comes time to buy or rent an apartment.

CHAPTER 3

THE RULES OF RENTING

If renting an apartment is your goal, your monthly wages and expenses will give you an idea of what you can afford to pay in rent. While you might be tempted to move outside your financial comfort zone should you find the "perfect" place and spend more than you can really afford, you should stick to your budget. No matter how much you love an apartment, the love will quickly fade if the expenses involved are too much for you to handle.

When considering where you want to live, think about how far the apartment is from work or school. If you drive, a long commute is both stressful and expensive. Living near public transportation can be a plus, but make sure you don't have to switch trains or buses so many times that you're exhausted before you reach your destination. Convenience also makes a difference when it comes to access to shopping, medical facilities, restaurants, parks, or whatever else is a priority for you. You'll want to take the crime rate into account, as well as your overall comfort level, as you walk through the neighborhood.

If you use public transportation, check that your apartment is located near the bus stop or train station to avoid making endless transfers to reach your destination.

A SMART SEARCH

There are many ways to look for an apartment, especially in the age of the Internet. Web sites such at HotPads.com, Realtor.com, and PadMapper.com, which includes listings from Craigslist, are laid out on a Google map. These sites can help you search based on neighborhood, price, number of bedrooms, and other features. You should also get the word out to friends and family in case anyone knows of a place that might suit your needs.

A real estate agent is another possible resource. He or she knows the area where you want to live and can weed out a lot of undesirable apartments, saving you a ton of time. Make certain you know about any fees upfront, however. Some real estate agents charge renters a fee once they sign a lease, while others charge that fee to the landlords.

The earlier you start searching, the better. You'll have a greater range of options and will feel less pressure to pick an apartment out of desperation, even though it fails to meet even your most basic requirements. If you have a lot of flexibility with your move-in date, winter is a great time to look for a rental. The combination of colder weather and the holidays keeps a lot of folks out of the market, which is good news for your apartment hunt.

INSIDE AND OUT

After you've narrowed down your choices, it's time to take a look at your potential apartment. If you're going to have a roommate, try to make sure that both of you are there for the

Before you decide on an apartment, take measurements to make sure that your bed, sofa, and other furnishings can fit comfortably within that space.

walk-through. Should that prove impossible, take plenty of pictures. A tape measure is a good idea, too, so you can be sure your bed or sofa and other large furniture will fit.

Beyond location, know what's most important in an apartment. It's a good idea to have a list written down so that you don't get wowed by something that's not on your list, while overlooking the absence of the crucial things that are on the list. A state-of-the-art stove is cool, but not if the bedroom is so small that you can barely turn around. Separate your must-haves—a laundry in the building, a place that allows pets—from things that are nice but not essential.

Make sure that you are thorough when checking out a potential home. Does the shower have good water pressure? Are bugs crawling around? What's the noise level like? The temperature? Are the hallways and grounds in decent shape? How about the neighbors? If you're single, do you feel comfortable being surrounded by families with young kids or older folks who might be a bit too interested in your comings and goings? Be honest with yourself and trust your gut before making a final decision.

LANDLORDS AND LEASES

There is a vital part of every rental apartment that has nothing to do with square footage or new bathroom fixtures: your relationship with your landlord (or the property manager in a larger complex owned by a management company). A landlord

HANDLING A DISPUTE WITH YOUR LANDLORD

IT'S NOT UNUSUAL FOR TENANTS AND LANDLORDS TO HAVE DISAGREEMENTS. COMMON SOURCES OF TENSION INCLUDE A TENANT'S FAILURE TO PAY RENT ON TIME, A LANDLORD'S REFUSAL TO FIX SOMETHING IN THE APARTMENT, AND DISPUTES OVER THE RETURN OF THE SECURITY DEPOSIT.

ONE WAY TO PROTECT YOURSELF AGAINST A DISPUTE OVER YOUR SECURITY DEPOSIT IS TO TAKE PICTURES OF THE APARTMENT BOTH WHEN YOU MOVE IN AND BEFORE YOU MOVE OUT. THESE PICTURES PROVIDE EVIDENCE OF THE APARTMENT'S CONDITION PRIOR TO YOUR TENANCY SHOULD YOUR LANDLORD CLAIM YOU CAUSED DAMAGE OR MADE MAJOR ALTERATIONS TO THE PLACE. IF YOU BELIEVE THE LANDLORD IS HOLDING ON TO YOUR SECURITY DEPOSIT UNFAIRLY, SEND HIM OR HER A NOTARIZED LETTER TO THAT EFFECT. IF YOU DON'T GET A SATISFACTORY RESPONSE, YOU CAN CONTACT YOUR LOCAL CONSUMER PROTECTION AGENCY, HOUSING AGENCY, OR TENANT OR APARTMENT ASSOCIATION. YOU CAN ALSO TAKE YOUR LANDLORD TO SMALL CLAIMS COURT SHOULD IT COME TO THAT.

ONCE YOU'VE SIGNED A LEASE SAYING YOU WILL PAY A CERTAIN AMOUNT OF RENT AT A CERTAIN TIME EACH MONTH, YOU NEED TO DO JUST THAT. YOU DON'T HAVE THE RIGHT TO HOLD BACK YOUR RENT FOR ANY REASON. SHOULD YOU FIND YOURSELF IN A TOUGH FINANCIAL SPOT FOR ONE MONTH, TALK TO YOUR LANDLORD. IN MANY CASES, IT'S EASIER FOR HIM OR HER TO WORK THINGS OUT WITH YOU THAN TO TRY AND FIND A NEW TENANT. IF YOU DON'T PAY YOUR RENT AT ALL, YOU COULD FACE EVICTION, WHICH IS A LAWSUIT BROUGHT BY THE LANDLORD TO

REMOVE YOU FROM THE APARTMENT. TAKING IN A ROOMMATE, BORROWING MONEY FROM A FRIEND OR FAMILY MEMBER, OR FINDING A NEW TENANT FOR THE APARTMENT ARE POSSIBLE FIXES FOR THIS VERY TOUGH SITUATION.

is the person who owns your apartment and your go-to person should you need anything fixed in your place.

Some landlords are very hands-off, which can work well as long as you don't have to pester him or her to get anything done. There are other landlords, however, who micromanage to the point where it feels intrusive, particularly if he or she lives near—or even in—the same building that houses your apartment. It's great to have someone nearby to deal with that overflowing toilet. It's not so great to have a landlord who pries into your personal or professional life. Try to get a sense of how your personalities will match up to save yourself trouble down the line.

The written agreement between a landlord and tenant is called a lease. Leases cover many items, including:

- The amount of rent due each month
- When that monthly rent is due
- Who will pay for utilities such as heat, hot water, and electricity (tenant or landlord)
- Whether you can have a pet in the apartment and any restrictions (size, type of animal) on that pet
- The maximum number of people allowed to live in the apartment
- How much notice you have to give the landlord before moving out

The lease will also cover how much you have to put down as a security deposit. This is money you give the landlord to protect him or her in case you fail to pay your rent or cause great damage to the apartment. A typical amount for a security deposit is one-and-a-half month's rent. If you've followed the terms of the lease, this money should be returned when your lease is up.

Make sure you read all the terms in your rental lease before signing it. Knowing your rights and responsibilities can help prevent disputes with your landlord later on.

While leases are binding, they are also negotiable. If there's something in the lease that you would like to change, talk to your landlord. Of course, you need to be reasonable. It's OK to ask that the weight limit on pets be moved from 10 pounds to 15 (4.5 kilograms to 6.8) or to try to have the landlord pay for one of the utilities. Asking him or her to cut your rent in half is unreasonable and unrealistic and will only cause tension in the relationship—or lead to you losing the apartment altogether.

You do have the right to expect your landlord to respond to your concerns about the apartment in a timely manner. The landlord should also give notice when he or she needs to enter the apartment to make repairs or to show the apartment to a prospective tenant. Many states have laws that protect your right to privacy. In general, however, leases are weighted in favor of the landlord, so it's up to you to make sure you're being treated fairly. That means reading your lease before you sign it and making sure that any other matter that's discussed is put in writing.

MYTHS AND FACTS

MYTH: IT'S ALWAYS BETTER TO OWN THAN TO RENT.

FACT: THERE ARE MANY FACTORS INVOLVED IN DECIDING WHETHER YOU SHOULD OWN VERSUS RENT AN APARTMENT, INCLUDING YOUR FINANCIAL SITUATION, THE CURRENT REAL ESTATE MARKET, AND YOUR PLANS FOR THE FUTURE. BUYING IS NOT ALWAYS THE BETTER CHOICE.

MYTH: WITH ALL THE INFORMATION AVAILABLE ON THE INTERNET, I DON'T NEED TO USE A REAL ESTATE AGENT TO FIND AN APARTMENT.

FACT: ALTHOUGH YOU MIGHT BE ABLE TO FIND AN APARTMENT WITHOUT AN AGENT, HE OR SHE CAN HELP GUIDE YOU, ESPECIALLY WHEN IT COMES TO THE COMPLICATED PROCESS OF BUYING AN APARTMENT.

MYTH: AS LONG AS I'M PAYING MY SHARE OF THE RENT, MY ROOMMATES SHOULD HAVE NO SAY OVER HOW I LIVE MY LIFE.

FACT: WHEN YOU LIVE WITH ROOMMATES, YOUR ACTIONS AFFECT EVERYONE IN THE APARTMENT. IF YOU'RE NOT PREPARED TO DEAL WITH A COOPERATIVE LIVING ENVIRONMENT, IT MIGHT BE BEST TO FIND YOUR OWN PLACE.

CHAPTER 4

SHARING AND SUBLETTING

There may come a time when you decide to share an apartment, either with your best friend, a friend of a friend, a sibling, a coworker, your boyfriend or girlfriend,

Whether you knew your roommate or roommates before you moved in together or met through an ad or roommate service, regular communication is the key to keeping things running smoothly.

or people you meet for the express purpose of sharing your living space. No matter what has brought you and your roommate together and why you've decided to share an apartment, you need to be both thoughtful and practical as you move forward.

You likely wouldn't have to look far to find someone with a horror story about a roommate situation gone wrong—rent not paid, relationships crushed, or that roommate who hogged the bathroom, clogged the sink, and thought nothing of blasting loud music at two AM. These are all situations that can transform your home from a safe haven into the last place you want to be. Although you can't avoid every rough spot, you can take steps to keep things as peaceful as possible.

THE RIGHT FIT

If you're looking to share an apartment with someone you don't know, a bit of research is in order. There are roommate-matching services such as Roommates.com and RoommateExpress.com that can help you find a compatible roommate in your area. Friends, family members, and coworkers are another good source of potential leads on promising roommates, as is your alumni association if you are a college graduate. Craigslist has a "rooms and shares" section as well, although the listings come without a personal reference or whatever screening a matching service might offer.

Whatever the source of a potential roommate, you have to do your own screening. Ask for work and personal references and search the Internet, including checking his or her Facebook page, Twitter account, and other social networking sites. If you're thinking about sharing with someone who already rents the apartment that you will move into, you still have the right to ask questions. Your safety and comfort level matter, too.

It's important to determine what you want in a roommate. Are you the quiet type who values calm and privacy above all? Or are you a social butterfly seeking the same in a roommate? How would you feel if your roommate had a very different schedule from you, working at night, perhaps, and sleeping during the day? Would it bother you if he or she had his significant other over several times a week? You have to know yourself in order to know what your ideal living situation would be—and what's a deal breaker.

SETTING UP HOUSE

No matter how well you screen or how compatible you think you are, no roommate situation is perfect. That's why it's vital to communicate with your roommate or roommates to keep a small problem from developing into a big one. Soon after you settle in, try to have a meeting to discuss the basics, including:

- How the monthly rent will be handled
- How utilities will be paid
- Whether buying and cooking food will be a shared responsibility or something each roommate handles separately
- How chores will be divided up
- The "house rules" on noise levels and overnight guests

In order to have a successful living experience, you have to treat your roommates with kindness and respect. If you know your roommate has to be at work an hour before you do, let him or her use the bathroom first in the morning. Make the effort to ask about her job or the movie he saw the night before. When it comes to his or her stuff, never "borrow" anything without permission or your roommate will feel like you can't be trusted.

If your roommate does something that bugs you, ask him or her to meet to discuss the issue at a time that's mutually convenient. Keep your comments specific to the latest incident (rather than launching into a laundry list of complaints dating back months) and avoid accusatory language. Instead, use language that focuses on your feelings ("I felt so stressed when I walked into the kitchen this morning and saw that you hadn't cleaned up after your meal") and leaves the door open for further discussion.

LIVING WITH A BFF OR SIGNIFICANT OTHER

Like most things, living with a close friend has its pluses and minuses. It's great to share an apartment with a person who knows you well and can follow what's going on in your life without being handed a cheat sheet. On the other hand, it's easy to fall into the trap of counting on your BFF to be the roommate version of one-stop shopping: a person to cook with and go to concerts with and someone who'll stay up until four in the morning discussing your job or love life because that's what friends are for.

Another potential problem is thinking there's no need to put anything in writing because a good friend would never stop paying rent or throw a party without letting you know first. In order to preserve the friendship, draw up a roommate agreement, keep the lines of communication open, respect each other's boundaries, and remember to give each other some much-needed space.

Moving in with a boyfriend or girlfriend is a big step. Before you cohabitate, make sure this is something you *both* want or there'll be tension from day one. If you do go ahead, you'll have to decide whether you're moving into his or her place, vice versa, or if you're getting a new place together. Talk through the pros and cons of each, and try not to rush the process.

In order to protect yourself and your partner, get both of your names on the lease. With that commitment set down on paper, you'll be able to focus on building a life with one another. This will likely take some adjustment. Habits that used to seem cute can become annoying when put under the microscope of daily life together. Not to mention all the *stuff* you both have, some of which will likely have to go into storage—or the Goodwill bin—when two households become one.

Try to be patient with each other, and talk often and openly about your concerns so that they don't turn into a crisis. You should also maintain outside interests and friendships. It's unhealthy to expect another person to fulfill your every need. By taking care of yourself, you'll have more energy for

---

If you're living with a close friend, boyfriend, or girlfriend, make sure to maintain your own interests and friendships. No one person can fulfill your every need.

LIVING WITH A SIBLING

SHARING AN APARTMENT WITH A BROTHER OR SISTER CAN OFFER MANY ADVANTAGES. YOU DON'T HAVE TO SEARCH CRAIGSLIST FOR A ROOMMATE, DO A BACKGROUND CHECK, OR WORRY THAT HE OR SHE WILL GIVE YOU TWO DAYS' NOTICE BEFORE MOVING OUT. THERE'S A SENSE OF TRUST BUILT UP OVER THE YEARS. ALTHOUGH YOU MIGHT NOT ALWAYS GET ALONG, YOU HAVE FAITH THAT YOU'LL WEATHER THE TOUGH TIMES BECAUSE YOU HAVE BEFORE.

AS WITH OTHER CLOSE RELATIONSHIPS, IT'S IMPORTANT TO MAINTAIN CLEAR BOUNDARIES. THIS COULD BE A PARTICULAR CONCERN WITH SIBLINGS, WHO MIGHT FEEL THAT THEY HAVE THE RIGHT TO COMMENT ON YOUR LIFE CHOICES. YOU NEED TO MAKE IT CLEAR THAT WHILE YOUR BROTHER OR SISTER'S CONCERN IS APPRECIATED, HIS OR HER MEDDLING IS NOT.

WHEN YOU'RE LIVING WITH A SIBLING, TRY TO SETTLE DISPUTES WITHOUT GETTING YOUR PARENTS INVOLVED. IF YOU RUN TO MOM OR DAD WHENEVER THERE'S AN ISSUE, YOU RUN THE RISK OF REPEATING CHILDHOOD PATTERNS THAT CAN PREVENT YOU FROM BECOMING A MATURE AND INDEPENDENT ADULT. TREAT THIS TIME WITH YOUR SIBLING AS A CHANCE TO PRACTICE HOW TO RESOLVE CONFLICTS, KNOWING THAT YOUR RELATIONSHIP WITH YOUR BROTHER OR SISTER IS FOREVER, REGARDLESS OF HOW MUCH STRAIN IT MAY ENDURE IN THE SHORT TERM. TRUSTING IN THE STRENGTH AND ENDURANCE OF THE SIBLING RELATIONSHIP MAKES IT EASIER TO BOTH EXPERIENCE CONFLICT AND RESOLVE IT.

your partner and more to share at the end of the day, which will help to keep your relationship strong.

SUBLETTING

When you sublet, you are renting an apartment from an absent tenant who then pays rent to his or her landlord. In this case,

Sublet situations can work well for all parties, as long everything is done aboveboard and there is a written agreement in place.

the tenant's name remains on the lease. Sublets can be a good option, particularly when you need to rent a place for less than a year. Just make sure that you are comfortable with all aspects of the situation.

Most sublets are legal as long as the tenant requests consent from the landlord in writing and includes details such as the start and end date of the lease, the reason for subletting, and the name and current address of the person subletting. The landlord cannot withhold his or her consent without a good reason for doing so.

Although the tenant is ultimately responsible for the lease, you still want to get everything down in writing. The last thing you want is the tenant showing up months ahead of time to reclaim his apartment or a landlord who resents your presence in the building. Make sure that the rent, the term of the lease (how long you'll be able to live in the apartment), and other important matters are ironed out before you sign any agreement.

10 GREAT QUESTIONS
TO ASK A REAL ESTATE PROFESSIONAL

1. How do I handle a landlord who keeps asking me overly personal questions?
2. How do I go about finding an apartment if I am moving to another part of the country?
3. Are there any government agencies that can help if I need assistance covering a month or two of rent?
4. Can I ask my roommate to pay more rent if his or her significant other is continually staying over in our apartment?
5. Do I have any recourse if the person who's subletting me his or her apartment comes back early and wants to kick me out?
6. Am I allowed to take pictures when I go to look at different apartments?
7. How many apartments should I look at before I decide on a place?
8. How do I get information on nearby schools in the area where I want to live?
9. How do I find out what my property tax will be on a certain apartment?
10. Does it make sense to pay my mortgage off early?

CHAPTER 5

WHEN YOU'RE READY TO BUY

Buying an apartment requires a huge investment of time, energy, and money. You need to think about the kind of home—and lifestyle—you want and then take the steps to make your dream a reality. It's important to remember, however, that you're unlikely to get everything you want in an apartment. That's why it's vital to know your priorities and do your research before making any decisions.

Maria Culato, author of *The Just Right Home*, suggests that you picture your life from the moment you wake up in the morning to the time you go to bed. This means thinking about not only how many bedrooms the apartment has, but also how much light the place lets in, how noisy the neighbors are, and whether there's a storage area for your extra belongings and a parking space for your car or bike. It's a good idea to write up a checklist of your needs and wants so that you have something to go by when you look at an apartment.

You're unlikely to get everything you want in an apartment, so be clear about which features matter most to you.

Of course, price has to be a big consideration when buying an apartment. How much of a down payment you can afford, along with the type of mortgage (home loan) you can get, affects which apartment you'll be able to purchase. According to CNNMoney.com, it is a good idea as a general rule to aim for a home that costs approximately two-and-a-half times your annual salary. To get some sense of your monthly payments for an apartment in your price range, you can use one of many online mortgage calculators.

KNOW THE NEIGHBORHOOD

Web sites such as Zillow.com, Realtor.com, and Trulia. com allow potential homebuyers to get details about an apartment without leaving their home. You can see pictures of the apartment and aerial maps of the neighborhood, too.

When considering a place to live, you want to make sure that you're moving into a thriving neighborhood so that your apartment retains its value. Beware of "For Sale" signs popping up everywhere because that probably means more people want to leave the area, rather than enter it. High-performing school districts matter, too, even for those residents without children. Good schools make a neighborhood desirable and help keep property values strong.

As with other aspects of the economy, the housing market fluctuates. In a buyer's market, there are more homes available than people to buy them, driving down prices and giving the buyer the advantage. When supply is low, prices

Make sure that the apartment you love is in a neighborhood that's thriving, with an active business district and few "For Sale" or "Going Out of Business" signs.

rise and the seller has the advantage. In a buyer's market, there is a risk in waiting for prices to go lower and lower. In time, prices will go up again, and you might find yourself suddenly shut out of an apartment that you wanted but waited too long to make an offer on.

In order to get some sense of how much apartments in your desired area cost, you can use the Zestimate feature on

Zillow.com or the "Not for Sale" section on Realtor.com. Type in an address, and you will find out the estimated value for not only that home but also other homes in the area, along with the square footage of the apartment, the year it was built, and other valuable information.

Once you have an idea of the type of home you want and can afford, you might want to meet with a lender before continuing your search. Although you won't get a mortgage on a particular property, the lender will go through your financial history and come up with an amount that it would be willing to loan you. The letter that states this amount is called a preapproval letter. With a preapproval letter from a mortgage lender, you'll have a good idea of how much you can afford, and sellers will take you more seriously as you look at various apartments.

THE RIGHT REALTOR

When you're ready to start looking at specific apartments, it's wise to have a real estate agent help you. Agents know the laws and customs of the area better than you do, which will help cut down your search time considerably. If you have friends or family who already live where you hope to buy an apartment, ask them for an agent recommendation. You might want to look for an agent who is a member of the National Association of Realtors. These agents have agreed to follow a code of ethics set out by the association.

CONDOS AND CO-OPS

Most apartments are either condominiums (condos) or co-operative apartments (co-ops). It's the ownership structure that gives these homes their name, not the layout or location (although most co-ops are found in larger cities). These homes

Condos and co-ops come in all shapes and sizes. The more amenities the building offers, the higher your maintenance fees will be.

can be in a high-rise or low-rise building or a town house or other dwelling.

When you own a condo, you have a mortgage and pay property taxes and have a deed to a particular apartment. Everything *inside* the condo is yours. Everything *outside* of your condo, called the common area, belongs to you and all the other condo owners. This includes the lobby, grounds, landscaping, health club/gym, and elevator, for example. When you buy a condo, you automatically become a member of the homeowners association and are required to pay dues to cover expenses associated with the common areas. Part of your dues will be put in a fund to cover larger projects, such as planting new bushes or repainting the outside of the building.

Condos typically cost less than single-family homes. The maintenance costs are cheaper because you are sharing these expenses with others in the homeowners association. You might also have access to extra features like a pool or gym that can be very expensive to add to a single-family home. On the downside, you aren't the only one deciding what color to paint the lobby or the outside of the building.

Both condos and co-ops have a board of directors, and both require lengthy and highly detailed financial applications from prospective buyers. Given the structure of a condo, with every buyer owning a deed to his or her home, condo boards tend to be more hands-off, with less impact on your day-to-day life. Evictions are rare.

A co-op has a different setup. A co-op owner does not have a deed to an individual apartment, but rather shares in the corporation that runs the building and obtains a lease that allows him or her to live in a certain unit of the building. Maintenance fees are higher in co-ops because they include property taxes. Rules tend to be more restrictive, too, covering everything from home decoration to when and how you can entertain. Also, since you are technically leasing the apartment, it is easier to get kicked out.

MAKE YOUR BEST OFFER

Once you find a home you want, it's time to make an offer to the seller. An offer to a seller spells out the terms of the deal, including:

- What you're willing to pay for the apartment
- What the real estate agent commission will be
- When you expect to close on, or take possession of, the apartment
- How much of the costs will be financed through a mortgage

The offer will likely include a way for you to opt out if you are not formally approved for a mortgage or if the apartment does not pass a home inspection.

Making an offer is a negotiating process. You shouldn't put out your highest offer first, but don't name a price so low that the seller won't take you seriously. If you've done your homework—and have a real estate agent you trust—you should be able to hit that sweet spot. That doesn't mean your offer will be accepted, however. There can be a lot of

When you make an offer to buy an apartment, don't come in at your upper limit. On the other hand, don't bid so low that the seller doesn't take you seriously.

back and forth when buying an apartment, and if others are interested in the same property, you could get into a bidding war.

It's important to focus on your needs and not get too caught up in the gamesmanship of it all. The best you can do is express your enthusiasm for the apartment, be reasonable, and offer an amount that stays within your financial comfort range. There's no point in owning an apartment that puts too much of a strain on your budget for you to enjoy living there.

TAKE A CLOSER LOOK

If your offer for an apartment is accepted, congratulations! Your journey is not over yet, however. The next step is to have a real estate lawyer draw up a formal contract stating that you intend to buy the apartment. Your lawyer will also likely go through your building's bylaws, rules, and renovation policies to make sure that everything is aboveboard and as expected. You don't want any last-minute surprises.

At the same time, you need to get the apartment inspected. You want to use someone who is not affiliated with either your real estate agent or your lender to make sure you get an independent and objective inspection report. A good resource is the American Society of Home Inspectors (ASHI), whose members must have performed at least 250 inspections and passed 2 proficiency exams to be certified.

THE MILLENNIAL HOUSING MARKET

FEW GROUPS HAVE BEEN HARDER HIT BY THE ECONOMIC DECLINE THAT BEGAN IN THE LATE 2000s THAN THE MILLENNIALS. BURDENED BY DEBT, FACING RECORD UNEMPLOYMENT, AND GREATLY AFFECTED BY THE VOLATILE HOUSING MARKET, THEY ARE PUTTING OFF MAJOR LIFE DECISIONS SUCH AS GETTING MARRIED OR HAVING A BABY. IN ADDITION, ACCORDING TO *ATLANTIC* MAGAZINE, 50 PERCENT FEWER AMERICANS ACQUIRED THEIR FIRST MORTGAGE BETWEEN 2008 AND 2011 COMPARED TO A DECADE BEFORE.

THIS GENERATION IS UNDERSTANDABLY CAUTIOUS. ANDREW BACA, WHO WORKS FOR THE SANDS CORPORATION, HAS PUT OFF BUYING A HOUSE BECAUSE OF THE STRUGGLING ECONOMY. "I COULD PURCHASE A HOME SOON," HE TOLD THE *LAS VEGAS REVIEW-JOURNAL*, "[B]UT I WOULD RATHER PAY DOWN DEBT AND SAVE, FOR LIQUIDITY AND SECURITY." THE DECISION TO PUT OFF BUYING A HOME NEGATIVELY AFFECTS NOT ONLY THE HOUSING MARKET, BUT ALSO THE MARKET FOR GOODS SUCH AS FURNITURE AND APPLIANCES. IF PEOPLE AREN'T BUYING HOUSES AND APARTMENTS, THEY ALSO AREN'T BUYING THINGS TO FILL THOSE HOMES, AND THE RIPPLE EFFECTS THROUGHOUT THE AILING ECONOMY SPREAD.

THIS CAUTION IS NOT ALL BAD, HOWEVER. TOO MANY PEOPLE BUYING HOUSES THEY COULDN'T AFFORD LED TO THE HOUSING BUST, AFTER ALL. MILLENNIALS SEEMED TO HAVE LEARNED AN IMPORTANT LESSON ABOUT FISCAL RESPONSIBILITY. THEY ARE EDUCATED ABOUT THE REAL ESTATE MARKET AND "VERY MUCH VALUE BUYERS," UNIVERSITY OF SOUTHERN CALIFORNIA SOCIAL-TREND

SCHOLAR **MOREY WINOGRAD** TOLD THE *LOS ANGELES TIMES.* THIS GENERATION IS INTERESTED IN ESSENTIALS, RATHER THAN LUXURY HOMES, AND THEY ARE WILLING TO BUY FIXER-UPPER HOUSES THAT THEY CAN UPGRADE THEMSELVES.

MORTGAGE MATTERS

Now that you know what apartment you plan to buy, it's time to go back to the lender to apply for a mortgage for that specific home. There are different types of mortgages available, so it's important to have a basic understanding of what certain terms mean.

A fixed-rate mortgage charges the same interest rate for the life of the loan, typically fifteen or thirty years. With a fixed-rate mortgage your payments never change, which helps when it comes to planning your monthly budget and can offer a sense of security. Fixed-rate mortgages charge higher interest rates, however, because the lender is taking a chance by offering you a long-term loan at a set rate. For example, if you lock in a thirty-year loan at an interest rate of 5 percent and interest rates go up to 10 percent, your lender loses money. On the other hand, if interest rates go way down, you lose out. The exception to this is if you refinance, which means getting a new mortgage to replace the old one. You have to qualify for a refinance loan, however, and there are fees involved.

An adjustable-rate mortgage (ARM) changes based on the current interest rate. This means it could go up or down depending on what's happening in the overall market. In most

Mortgage Rates

Rates as of 1/9/11

30-Year Fixed

4.750 Rate

4.953 APR

1.500 Points

Monthly Payment

3.375

3.357

1.000

> With a fixed-rate mortgage, your interest rate stays the same for the life of the home loan, which is typically fifteen or thirty years. Adjustable rate mortgages, on the other hand, are subject to the up-and-down fluctuations of interest rates.

cases, ARMs are adjusted every six or twelve months, but it could be more often depending on your terms. As ARMs can go up or down, they are a riskier bet and could make a real mess of your budget. Lenders know you are taking a risk with this type of mortgage, so they will likely charge you a lower interest rate than you would get with a fixed-rate mortgage for the first year or two. If you are planning to stay in your apartment for only a short time, the initial low interest of an ARM could work in your favor. Over the long life of a loan, however, if rates go up more than a couple of percentage points, an ARM will cost you more.

When deciding on the length of your mortgage, remember that a fifteen-year mortgage will require higher monthly payments but will be paid off sooner, which will cost less in the end. Your mortgage professional can help you with all aspects of your home loan, but you should never feel pressured into taking out a certain type of mortgage or a mortgage for more money than you are comfortable borrowing. You are the one who has to pay it back after all.

CLOSING THE DEAL

Within three days of applying for a loan, you should receive a Good Faith Estimate (GFE), which will provide you with details about the terms of your loan, as well as what you can expect to pay for various types of insurance and taxes. All these numbers can be overwhelming, but it's vital for you to know what kind of offer you're getting, given that you'll be paying off your mortgage for years to come.

The closing is when you give the seller money, and the seller gives you the title to the property, which means you legally own the apartment (or shares in the association and the right to live in a specific apartment if it's a co-op building). Both you and the seller should be present, as well as your lawyers and real estate agents, who will be collecting their commission

at this point. You will owe a good chunk of money at the closing, including your down payment, a portion of your mortgage, lawyer's fees, and other costs.

Owning an apartment can bring great happiness and a sense of pride, provided that you continue to live within your means. Although you might want to redecorate or even remodel slightly—if that's allowed in your building—stick to your monthly budget and remember that unexpected costs are bound to arise. A new couch is lovely. A visit from the plumber to fix a stubborn clog in your drain is a necessity. If you put the same effort into maintaining your apartment as you did into finding it, it should be yours to enjoy for as long as you choose to make it your home.

Getting the keys to your new place marks the beginning of an important life milestone, one that requires financial planning, prudence, and intelligence. Living in a home that you can afford and that suits your needs and lifestyle will lead to an exhilarating sense of freedom, independence, security, and happiness.

affiliated Closely connected to a particular group or organization.

austerity Measures taken to cut down on spending in order to save money and stay within a certain budget.

bankruptcy The legal process that a person goes through when he or she is not able to repay his or her debts.

bylaw The law or rule that governs how a homeowners association manages a property.

cohabitate An arrangement in which two people who are intimately involved decide to live together on a permanent basis.

common area Part of a property that is open to all who live there.

credential A qualifications or achievement that makes someone suitable for a particular job.

deed A legal document that transfers ownership of real estate from one party to another.

ethics Moral principles that guide the way a person conducts his or her private and professional life.

eviction A legal process by which a tenant is forced out of a property.

gamesmanship Strategies used to gain a psychological advantage when playing a game.

inflation An overall increase in prices for goods and services.

intrusive Causing disruption or discomfort due to unwanted attention.

investigate Looking into a particular situation in order to gather facts and details.

investment property A piece of real estate that a person or group puts money into with the expectation of making a profit over time.

miscellaneous Made up of a collection of various and unrelated types of people or things.

negotiable Open to discussion and modification in order to reach an agreement.

priority The factor that is most important when making a decision.

recourse A means of getting help in a difficult situation, including by legal means.

suburban Having to do with a small and/or residential community on the outskirts of a larger city.

Canada Mortgage and Housing Corporation (CMHC)
700 Montreal Road
Ottawa, ON K1A 0P7
Canada
(800) 668-2642
Web site: http://www.cmhc.ca
The Canada Mortgage and Housing Corporation is the
national housing agency of Canada. It works to enhance
financing opportunities for those wishing to own a home.

Canadian Housing & Renewal Association (CHRA)
75 Albert Street, Suite 902
Ottawa, ON K1P 5E7
Canada
(613) 594-3007
Web site: http://www.chra-achru.ca
The Canadian Housing & Renewal Association works to
make sure that all Canadians have access to an affordable,
secure, and decent place to call home.

Consumer Financial Protection Bureau (CFPB)
P.O. Box 4503
Iowa City, IA 52244
(855) 411-2372
Web site: http://www.consumerfinance.gov
The Consumer Financial Protection Bureau provides infor-
mation on mortgages, school loans, credit card debt, and
other consumer financial products.

Institute for Financial Literacy
260 Western Avenue, Suite 1
South Portland, ME 04106
(207) 221-3663
Web site: https://financiallit.org
The mission of the Institute for Financial Literacy is to promote effective financial education and counseling.

Jump$tart Coalition for Personal Financial Literacy
National Headquarters
919 18th Street NW, Suite 300
Washington, DC 20006
(888) 45-EDUCATE (338-2283)
Web site: http://www.jumpstart.org
This coalition of organizations shares an interest in advancing financial literacy among students in pre-kindergarten through college.

National Fair Housing Alliance (NFHA)
1101 Vermont Avenue NW, Suite 710
Washington, DC 20005
(202) 898-1661
Web site: http://www.nationalfairhousing.org
The National Fair Housing Alliance works to eliminate housing discrimination and ensure housing opportunity for all people through leadership, education, outreach, membership services, public policy initiatives, advocacy, and enforcement.

National Low Income Housing Coalition (NLIHC)
727 15th Street NW, 6th Floor
Washington, DC 20005
(202) 662-1530
Web site: http://www.nlihc.org
The National Low Income Housing Coalition advocates for
low-income families in need of safe and affordable housing.

U.S. Department of Housing and Urban Development (HUD)
451 7th Street SW
Washington, DC 20410
(202) 708-1112
Web site: http://www.hud.gov
The U.S. Department of Housing and Urban Development
provides information on mortgages, home inspections,
tenants rights, and other issues relevant to those buying or
renting a home.

WEBSITES

Due to the changing nature of Internet links, Rosen Publishing
has developed an online list of websites related to the subject
of this book. This site is updated regularly. Please use this link
to access the list:

http://www.rosenlinks.com/FSLS/Apart

Bailey, Adam Leitman. *Finding the Uncommon Deal: A Top New York Lawyer Explains How to Buy a House for the Lowest Possible Price.* Hoboken, NJ: Wiley, 2011.

Baron, Leonard P. *Buying a House, Condo, or Townhome.* Seattle, WA: CreateSpace, 2011.

Bray, Ilona, Alayna Schroeder, and Marcia Stewart. *Nolo's Essential Guide to Buying Your First Home.* 4th ed. Berkeley, CA: Nolo 2012.

Chatzky, Jean. *Money Rules: The Simple Path to Lifelong Security.* Emmaus, PA: Rodale Books, 2012.

Cusato, Marianne, and Daniel DiClerico. *The Just Right Home: Buying, Renting, Moving—or Just Dreaming—Find Your Perfect Match!* New York, NY: Workman Publishing, 2013.

Davidoff, Howard. *The Everything Personal Finance in Your 20s and 30s Book.* Avon, MA: Adams Media, 2012.

Guttentag, Jack. *The Mortgage Encyclopedia.* 2nd ed. New York, NY: McGraw-Hill, 2010.

Hodges, Jane. *Rent vs. Own: A Real Estate Reality Check for Navigating Booms, Busts, and Bad Advice.* San Francisco, CA: Chronicle Books, 2012.

Kennedy, Mark: *How to Buy a House the Right Way.* Seattle, WA: CreateSpace, 2012.

Khalfani-Cox, Lynnette. *Perfect Credit: 7 Steps to a Great Credit Rating.* Mountainside, NJ: Advantage World Press, 2010.

KMS Publishing. *Before You Rent: Your Ultimate Guide on Rental Advice for House Renting and Apartment Renting.* Seattle, WA: CreateSpace, 2010.

Kobliner, Beth. *Get a Financial Life: Personal Finance in Our Twenties and Thirties*. New York, NY: Simon & Schuster, 2009.

Leeds, Regina. *One Year to an Organized Financial Life*. Boston, MA: DaCapo Press, 2009.

Mazor, Pat, and Georgene Harkness. *Mortgage Rips-Offs: Learn the Secret to Saving Thousands Before You Apply*. Seattle, WA: CreateSpace, 2013.

Mundis, Jerrold. *How to Get Out of Debt, Stay Out of Debt, and Live Prosperously*. Revised ed. New York, NY: Bantam Books, 2012.

Orman, Suze. *The Money Book for the Young, Fabulous, and Broke*. New York, NY: Riverhead Trade, 2007.

Orman, Suze. *The Money Class: How to Stand in Your Truth and Create the Future You Deserve*. New York, NY: Spiegel & Grau, 2012.

Peebles, Noel. *Should I Buy a Home: Rent vs. Buy*. Seattle, WA: Amazon Digital Services, 2012.

Reed, David. *Financing Your Condo, Co-op, or Townhouse*. New York, NY: AMACOM, 2009.

Siegel, Cary. *Why Didn't They Teach Us This in School?* Seattle, WA: CreateSpace, 2013.

Siegel, Dale Robyn. *The New Rules for Mortgages*. New York, NY: Alpha Books, 2009.

Tyson, Eric. *Mortgages for Dummies*. 3rd ed. Hoboken, NJ: Wiley, 2011.

Tyson, Eric. *Personal Finance in Your 20s for Dummies.* Hoboken, NJ: Wiley, 2011.

Vaz-Oxlade, Gail. *Debt-Free, Forever: Take Control of Your Money and Your Life.* New York, NY: The Experiment LLC, 2010.

Warner, Ralph, Toni Ihara, and Frederick Hertz. *Living Together: A Legal Guide for Unmarried Couples.* 15th ed. Berkeley, CA: Nolo, 2013.

Weston, Liz. *Your Credit Score.* 4th ed. Upper Saddle River, NJ: FT Press, 2011.

Brown, Meta, et al. "Grading Student Loans." Federal Reserve Bank of New York, March 5, 2012. Retrieved November 2013 (http://libertystreeteconomics.newyork fed.org/2012/03/grading-student-loans.html).

Brown, Meta, et al. "Press Briefing on Household Debt and Credit." Federal Reserve Bank of New York, February 28, 2013. Retrieved November 2013 (http://liberty streeteconomics.newyorkfed.org/2013/02/just-released -press-briefing-on-household-debt-and-credit.html).

Chopra, Rohit. "Student Loan Debt Swells, Federal Loans Now Top a Trilion." Consumer Financial Protection Bureau, July 17, 2013. Retrieved November 2013 (http://www.consumerfinance.gov/newsroom/student -debt-swells-federal-loans-now-top-a-trillion).

Cusato, Marianne. *The Just Right Home*. New York, NY: Workman Publishing, 2013.

Kaufman, Joanne. "Mom Always Said to Share." *New York Times*, March 1, 2013. Retrieved November 2013 (http://www.nytimes.com/2013/03/03/realestate/ siblings-as-roommates-mom-always-said-to-share .html).

Lerner, Michelle. "How This Couple Got Rid of $136,000 in Debt in 21 Months." *Business Insider*, May 31, 2013. Retrieved November 2013 (http://www.businessinsider .com/we-got-rid-of-136000-in-debt-in-21 -months-2013-5).

Lowrey, Annie. "Student Debt Slows Growth as Young Spend Less." *New York Times*, May 10, 2013. Retrieved

November 2013 (http://www.nytimes.com/2013/05/11/business/economy/student-loan-debt-weighing-down-younger-us-workers.html).

Martin, Andrew, and Andrew W. Lehren. "A Generation Hobbled by the Soaring Cost of College." *New York Times*, May 12, 2012. Retrieved November 2013 (http://www.nytimes.com/2012/05/13/business/student-loans-weighing-down-a-generation-with-heavy-debt.html).

Milevsky, Moshe A. *Is Buying a Home or Renting Right for You?* Upper Saddle River, NJ: Pearson Education, 2010.

Orman, Suze. *The Money Class*. New York, NY: Spiegel & Grau, 2012.

Parker, Kim. "The Boomerang Generation." Pew Research Center, 2012. Retrieved November 2013 (http://www.pewsocialtrends.org/2012/03/15/the-boomerang-generation).

Quealy, Kevin, and Archie Tee. "Is It Better to Buy or Rent?" *New York Times*. Retrieved November 2013 (http://www.nytimes.com/interactive/business/buy-rent-calculator.html).

Reckard, E. Scott. "Are Millennials a Window of Opportunity or a Closed Door for Home Builders?" *Los Angeles Times*, June 7, 2013. Retrieved November 2013 (http://articles.latimes.com/2013/jun/07/business/la-fi-house-debt-20130607).

Rhodes, Trevor. *American Tenant*. New York, NY: McGraw-Hill, 2009.

Robinson, Jennifer. "Millennials Wary of Buying First Home." *Las Vegas Review-Journal*, August 10, 2013. Retrieved November 2013 (http://www.reviewjournal.com/business/economy/many-millennials-wary-first-home-purchase).

Stellin, Susan. "The Formidable Co-op Approval Process." *New York Times*, December 20, 2012. Retrieved November 2013 (http://www.nytimes.com/2012/12/23/realestate/getting-started-preparing-for-the-co-op-approval-process.html).

Stewart, Marcia. "How to Find a Good Apartment." Nolo.com. Retrieved November 2013 (http://www.nolo.com/legal-encyclopedia/free-books/renters-rights-book/chapter1-5.html).

Thompson, Derek. "The Unluckiest Generation: What Will Become of Millennials?" *Atlantic*, April 26, 2013. Retrieved November 2013 (http://www.theatlantic.com/business/archive/2013/04/the-unluckiest-generation-what-will-become-of-millennials/275336).

Tyson, Eric, and Ray Brown. *Home Buying Kit for Dummies*. 5th edition. Hoboken, NJ: Wiley, 2012.

U.S. Department of Education. "Federal Student Aid Strategic Plan Fiscal Years 2012–2016." Retrieved November 2013 (http://www2.ed.gov/about/offices/list/fsa/fiveyearplan.pdf).

ABOUT THE AUTHOR

Jennifer Landau received her M.A. degree in creative writing from New York University and her M.St. in general and special education from Fordham University. An experienced editor, she has also published nonfiction books. Recent titles include *Bipolar Disorder* and *Cybercitizenship: Online Rights and Responsibilities*.

PHOTO CREDITS

Cover, p. 3 Peter Dazeley/Photographer's Choice/Getty Images; pp. 6–7 Image Source/Getty Images; p. 10 Justin Sullivan /Getty Images; p. 13 Peter Cade/Iconica/Getty Images; p. 15 Bartek Szewczyk/iStock/Thinkstock; p. 18 Purestock/Thinkstock; p. 21 © David Young-Wolff/PhotoEdit; p. 22 © AP Images; p. 25 PRNewsFoto/MassMutual/AP Images; p. 31 UpperCut Images/Getty Images; p. 33 PM Images/The Image Bank/Getty Images; p. 37 © Kayte Deioma/PhotoEdit; p. 40 Tom Merton/Caiaimage/Getty Images; p. 45 Burger/Phanie /SuperStock; p. 47 The Boston Globe/Getty Images; p. 51 Izabela Habur/E+/Getty Images; p. 53 Stephen Saks/Lonely Planet Images/Getty Images; p. 55 Tyson Wirtzfeld/E+ /Getty Images; p. 58 Noel Hendrickson/Blend Images/Getty Images; p. 62 Juanmonino/E+/Getty Images; p. 64 Caspar Benson/Getty Images; interior page design elements © iStock photo.com/yystom (arrows), © iStockphoto.com/JLGutierrez (financial terms), © iStockphoto.com/ahlobystov (numbers).